THE DECLARABLE FUTURE

FOUR LAKES POETRY SERIES

THE DECLARABLE FUTURE

JENNIFER BOYDEN

The University of Wisconsin Press

The University of Wisconsin Press
1930 Monroe Street, 3rd Floor
Madison, Wisconsin 53711-2059
uwpress.wisc.edu

3 Henrietta Street
London WC2E 8LU, England
eurospanbookstore.com

Printed in the United States of America

Library of Congress Cataloging-in-Publication Data
Boyden, Jennifer.
The declarable future / Jennifer Boyden.
p. cm. — (Four Lakes poetry series)
Poems.
ISBN 978-0-299-29214-0 (pbk. : alk. paper)
ISBN 978-0-299-29213-3 (e-book)
I. Title. II. Series: Four Lakes poetry series.
PS3602.O9344D43 2013
811'.6—dc23
2012032681

For Gavia

CONTENTS

ACKNOWLEDGMENTS

Grateful acknowledgment to the editors of the following publications in which these poems first appeared, often in different forms:

Orion: "They Have a Point"

Beloit Poetry Journal: "The Person with the Loupe"

American Poetry Journal: "As If I Hadn't Worn It Quite Enough, Time Tattoos My Arms and Face" and "Bad Advice"

The Gettysburg Review: "The Declarable Future"

The Adirondack Review: "The Misunderstanding of Wool"

Folio: "David on the Phone"

Gadfly: "The Lost Man Thanks the Curtains"

Rattle: "You Might Have Mentioned How the Doorknobs Worked"

Poets Against the War: "Counting the Dead"

Cimarron Review: "The Magician"

Twenty Views of Cascade Head: "Each Answer Addresses the Previous Answer"

basalt: "In This Place, Which We Have Been" and "The Lost Man Leaves a Will"

I offer ever increasing thanks to Ron Wallace for the delight of this series, which springs, no surprise, from his own delightful self. I am also deeply thankful for Nance Van Winckel and those who join her in carrying invisible flotation devices with them everywhere: John Bisbee, Janice King, Monte Riggs, and Weston Cutter. Thanks also to Sam Hamill for pointing to the path, Kennon McKee for room to write, Rebeckah B. Turner for submissions magic, and Adam Mehring for his better-making editorial self. And to Ian and Gavia, for the multitudes.

In an alleyway beside a nightclub
a miniature figure is vomiting;

that's how you know this is no
ordinary snowglobe.
　　　　—Tony Hoagland

Millions were dead; everybody was innocent.
　　　　—Charles Simic

1.

YOU MIGHT HAVE MENTIONED
HOW THE DOORKNOBS WORKED

The doorknobs were made of crystal. We found out
later they were what transmitted the filament voices
we heard. The voices grew weak when late-night
static ripped the words at their seams, but morning
repaired the voices, and they started in again.

The voices told us to buy clothes for ourselves,
cover our bodies with lotion, find salvation,
but we could not find the speaking body. We burned
sage in the corners and got up in the night to find
what sang, what asked,
what said and said and said.

Mornings, our children woke to find us sleeping
on silent lawns because we'd emptied the indoor
mattresses like stomachs. Always in search of the voices.
Then we'd head inside again to where sounds swelled
across our breakfast: a horse crossed the finish line,
the president was up to something, a cello
darkened the frame.

The only one unbothered was the neighbor
who understood it was finally the angels speaking.
He'd always wanted to know the answers to things.
Now, he understood why prices were down,
the Sox were trading up, the roads would need repair.

Sometimes, pausing at his threshold, he heard it best:
how the world was behaving out there and what to look for.
He heard how sunsets were expanded
by the silt of exhaust and what women should wear
underneath.

He likely pitied the way the rest of us searched our houses,
looked inside each vase, each cup, the boots, gutted
our couches: *You in there?*

The voices came from somewhere, and they wanted to include us.
This was how we understood it.
This is what the voices said.

SMALL GIFTS ARE THOUGHTFUL, BUT REQUIRE ACCEPTANCE OF THE WORLD'S DISMANTLEMENT

First, the feather left next to my plate.
And later, a ribbon tied to the window latch.
Gifts that meant I had been remembered.

They seemed messages though of falling, of absence—
the bird no longer attached to its feather,
the ribbon's gift no longer within.

It used to be that small offerings were enough
to convince me to stay:
leaf of a jade plant, rough stone left on my pillow,
gold clasp left to gather the sun.

The clasp, already once broken from its former purpose
of closure. Now, air on one side, air on the other,
it binds one half the splitting world to the other.

And the stone, taken from its ancestry of cliff
and breakage, will never be returned to that story.

                    I am concerned
with removal and loss.

If you must leave
a gift, do not let it be one thing taken from another.

NIGHT PITCH

Midnight, and I'm up another night
to stumble into the hallway as if it's the earth
that needs to steady itself—the earth with a glitch
deep in the underearth gears where the machinery
hesitates and then slides back into position
so people like me who are up at midnight
can walk without leaning against the wall.

The gear inside the earth's turning
didn't used to get checked much
because sleeping used to come easy
in this part of the world—before everyone started
walking around with a soldier of their own to bury
and chemo tattoos and a firm understanding
of the best dish detergent for washing
the ruined birds.

You know the birds die anyway, right?
If that's what's waking me up at night, I should keep it
to myself. Because it is gratuitous to state out loud
that the ocean is sad and so requires my sleep, as if
the whole town isn't black-eyed
with waking, making it clear that another night
of tossing and wandering doesn't make me unique.
This oceanic despair. Salt to salt. Water to wave.

Waking at midnight, we make it just in time
to the night window where it's our own faces
staring back at us, faces that bob like life rafts
on the glass of ocean.

And since we're up and paying attention,
the earth has to do its thing: all that turning
just so we can get some peace and stumble back to sleep.
Nothing out of the ordinary here, we say,
the earth's still turning. As if we could handle
one more shock anyway.

The earth is generous like that: Won't have us
thinking it takes a rest, the way it did
for all those years when it was flat and full of bones
from The Ark. Once the world began its spinning,
the stars were sort of along for the ride.
Fixed, of course, but for us they make it look easy,
like they're still up to the old business
of telling stories and predicting crops.

As further proof of the world's kindness,
the toilet swirls reliably to the right,
and the refrigerator spits out another cube.
It's the world we know, on cue. By the time night is over

the dog is hopeful, because getting up
means morning, and morning means food
when everyone is awake and tipping toward the center
of the house which is always the kitchen.

Then the lights going on across the street start
the waterfall. We all know
that when the stream begins to run
in the front yard over there, the people must be
home. They look tired. Exhausted, really,
though I didn't know they cared much about air
or pelicans. They aren't the type who believe
in particulate matter or dark matter or matters
smaller than their Toyota Sequoia, interestingly parked
half up on the curb as if the street, tree lined
and tolerant of U-turns, isn't nearly enough.
They want the grass of the parking strip too.

We all want the grass, I suppose. Thick
with hard edges sliced off at the curb
where the message is clear: I made this,
and it's a line.
A line is a good start—
don't get me wrong. The line is the beginning
of art, really. It's also the marker between a challenge

and a fight. In art as in challenges,
how one crosses the line is really the only thing
that matters when considered afterward.

If I have to admit it, the neighbors look like hell.
As if the face they saw in last night's window
is the one that watched their childhood
when all the blinds were drawn.
The face that knows of the world's dwindling,
and knows there won't be more. And therefore,
we have concluded by law, children should not be
out of bed past hours. They need to learn
there won't always be span enough of world to roam
from one side of night to the other.

Back to bed, where the world can hang on
to its edges—the edges, which do not come
with a primer in how to get a good stream going
with fully adjustable dimmer switch
and waterfalls with proven removable filters.
When the world we know disappears,
we have been assured, we can ride the ocean rafts
of plastic, catalogue the shapes that glide beneath,
and test our blood for cells.

THE GIANT

His huge clothes feeble and haul the line,
spent as the woman who struggles to hang
them. The wet pants, wide as a banquet,
slap and stick, while

inside, her giant on his bed, trying to lift
his head to see an original patch of sky,
a hillside of world.

He can see it better on the screen: erase
and carve, erode and melt.
The woman has told him when the time comes
she will not leave him.

He can become her life raft
when the melt of glaciers rises, every shirt
a sail.

She has it planned: the small people
will huddle atop him, her man outstretched,
floating, an offering she can make
because the world is broken,
the man she's grown adrift and useful as an island.

THE MISUNDERSTANDING OF WOOL

As if animals aren't terrified of the blades
of their shearing. In the thrift stores, it is easy to see
how the wool of this town has been misunderstood.

Hung with shrunken woolens, the racks display their ruins:
sailor pants, the funeral suits, hats
for shrunken heads, and heat-tightened sweaters.

When I have assembled the pile, I begin to teach the wool
the old ways of their sheep and rabbits.
I remove false eyes of pearl buttons, cut the tags
of secondary origins. And then

I teach them heartbeat and bunching into corners, teach them
grass height for hiding and grass green for food, hawk
shadow, owl call, magpie lures and mimics.

The dry woolens must be reintroduced to oil
if they are to make it. They will need to be given back
to fear of the coming dog and of bramble snags.

They must never trust water or anything that beckons
with the reflection of ourselves.

FOR THE CHURCH SINGERS
ON HOWARD AND JUNIPER

I heard the squirrel dying somewhere under a street wire.
High mewling, the crushed call of it asking to be smashed
quickly with a rock so we could all get back
to our Sunday of moving plants to the other side of the yard
and adjusting the trees for better reception.

There was no squirrel. At the end of the voice I followed,
a church on Juniper and Howard where nothing was dying
except the art of song, lifted by voices on a tilting tin plate
as an offering to a god of worship. The god of no ears.
The god of why bother, of make it stop, of use silence
to let me know when it's over.

Voices thin-glassed as a light bulb, dim filament shine
of song inside. Raised high to the god of my gratitude
for what was not the squirrel of that morning's prayer.

THEY HAVE A POINT

When the gods gave us all the holes
leading into our darkness, they planned
on our needing a mystery. It amuses them
that what is inside the body
is more body. The same body, but different.

They first said the bodies should be mostly moss inside.
But they kept coming back to the mystery.

Though they liked that moss would have kept everyone
soft and green, they decided it was best
to fill each thing with itself, which would then be hidden
within the other. *Look at stones*, they said.
Look at water which is like a throat of water.

THE LOST MAN MEETS THE GIANT

The water kept rising, crops under, cars under,
high ground a low note, and not a boat gone by.
The lost man had seen it happen before: the people wanted
water, and so they were given water.
One by one, they became what they asked for,
until he was alone and clinging.
Eventually, the land returned
because that was also asked, and the lost man
stepped down onto it.

But this time, no one had asked for water.
It came anyway. Then everyone asked for land,
but it did not answer. The trees were tired.
The animals barely had enough left over
to kill each other, and they slept in gray branches.
Then the giant floated under with arms spread so wide
the invitation was hardly a question,
and the lost man jumped aboard.

The woman who handed him a pole
gave him a quadrant to work and went back to her area.
Along the way, the lost man pulled in chickens
and fruit from the trees, slaughtered hogs
in the Knee Region of the Giant,
fed strips and chunks into Territory of the Mouth.

The giant's hunger was their only strategy.
It floated them. It grew by feeding.

At night they lit fires on barrel floats and told stories.
One of them whispered that in all the stories,
the raft's demise is what determines the next chapter
for its people. *And there is always*, says the man, *a demise*.
They will need a plan.

The lost man shapes his plan's story with his hands.
He acts a tree, shows a harvesting of branches
and a lashing of them together. He still believes
trees might save them. The woman says no.
She knows her giant, and hunger's question
will never surprise them with a different answer.
They will be fine, she says, as long as
they can gather birds and seals, lure exhausted deer.

As long as they can cull the matted sheep, the swirling
cats, as long as they can pull seaweed, reel fish,
follow riptides through to pelicans and cormorants,
find canisters of wheat, haul in bears with grapple hooks,
hack meat out of turtles, empty the ocean's bag
of fish. As long as that, then that.

EACH ANSWER ADDRESSES
THE PREVIOUS ANSWER

All day, river pull and ocean pull
against the log caught between them.

A spin toward the river. Another
toward the sea.

It goes on like this and the moon
is faint in the sky,

a promise to help the tide decide
where to place its catch.

No one is next to me to say how
it will end. The flowers

all around have been in bloom for some time,
and their scent fades with the light.

LIKE A FREQUENCY, LIKE LOOKING RIGHT AT IT

In June, the man noticed how quietly the evenings held
themselves. Birds did not have to ask to continue, nor
the grass. There were no answers anyway that meant
they could not do as they wished, and so flying, and so
the world greenly.

The man could not say he didn't want such a silent, green world
to continue for all of us, and he still says it is acceptable to go on
as if the trees will never let go of the sky.
But when one pine is cut, the man read somewhere,

the ones left behind increase their own production
of sap. However the trees know it,
the cutting changes them. The man didn't plan to leave.
He might have stayed, despite.
But the rest of what is happening—far away, in great blasts—
is also happening within the man's chest, is happening

now, including what goes unmentioned. Either way,
poems make poor baskets: they hold what they leave out
as well as what they keep.

Of June, the silence around the other world was not a grace:
it was time holding itself in its own arms
because to let go would mean the great unraveling. The birds
were the least of it.

The birds had made it nearly possible to stay. But
because everything else went on as if, the man left it behind,
looking for something small enough to go unnoticed
so he might never have to give it up.

THE BODY, BEING MOSTLY WATER

Every night we try again:
he from the lake that lost him, and I
drinking its water.
There will be nothing closer
than how he swims in my throat. Bite
of green water. Tongue's sift of the silt
that darkens the floor of his last boat,
his body of dissolve spread across
a floor no grapnel drag can translate.
In my body, the cells
receive him, each rimmed
in the slip of an edge he cannot grasp
and so he drowns again.
I want to hear how his voice ushers
to the reeds. I want to spread
into something so clear
strangers could wash
their hands in my transparency.
I want to undress sediment
before sleep. I need to count his teeth.

THE DECLARABLE FUTURE

Cousins, is it possible
we have misunderstood the mud?
Is it alright to assert that the sturgeon found
the rift in time and swam through it toward us?

What is it you know, today? Somewhere, a bird
is calling me, though I haven't yet learned
what to call me. Inside, something is absorbent.
Inside, the curves are not judicious.

Cousins, we are here in an assemblage of days
that appear to come one right after the other.
The supreme order of this-and-then-the-next is exquisite
if you need that kind of thing.

I cannot remember what the molds were for.
There were things poured into them, but no one wanted
to claim what came out. I am sure of that.
And I am also sure no one sent the letter about how
it was all a misunderstanding, how leotards and snowglobes

and dangling cords were just a walk that took a bad turn
onto a very long road. Dolphins can recognize themselves,
which means they have a self they are aware of.
This is science. The rest of it is what we suspect

we're talking about from the steps of our porches,
though I have never quite learned where you live.

2.

DAVID ON THE PHONE

David sober says to feed the bear
who's eating the birdseed in my front yard.
Says I must, for him, feed it so I'll earn a badge
under the god he's wearing lately. God with eyes.
God who sleeps a lot when David needs him most,
and whose waking patience is thin
as the bear's winter cells. This god of tallying
and disappearances is called upon by David most
in the time of morning vapor when it's hardest
for David sober to believe: whole day stretched
in front of him like paint thinner, each cup a cup
which is to be used for coffee only. Feed the bear,
David says sober though alone at his end of the hour
when the god might wake for him. David says
it would go well for all of us if only I pour milk over bread,
honey over meat, and then carry out the bowl.
But lock the door when you're back in, David says
sober, because the source is always sweeter
than the meal. He says the bear's salvation will be heard
and might speak for him at the end of his need.

And with what sweetness on the tongue
will it urge the god of that single cup awake?
And with what honeyed breath will it seek
me out again, small god terrified of the asking?

THE BOOK OF VARIOUS STUDIES

1.
When the gods finally understand that too many people
know the same things, they decree that each person
should find a specialty.

The people race to claim dinosaurs, white wine, tide pools.
But the gods allow only one person per item.
By dusk the streets are sparse with the few left looking
for what to love enough
to become their life of inquiry.

The pearl button, suggest the gods hopefully, *has been sadly
overlooked*. They go on to note that no one
chose the arrival of four p.m. or the absence of candles
in the park.

The man who continually learns his first choice
has just been taken decides to study his wife, but someone
else was already approved for her. He'd make a child
so he could study that, but the rules are against it.

He hopes the person who has chosen to study him
won't see how he has been left with nothing,
but he never sees anyone following him no matter
how bright the night or deserted the alley he hides in.

2.

In his pocket, he finds a grain of sand he first mistook
for a stone. But when he calls it stone, the word
wavers in his mouth. He applies to have the question
of stone versus sand as his study, and this is granted
by the gods.

        By microscope, the man observes

the stony countenance: abrupt angles, an ancestry of gray.
Though in his hand, he can feel how it needs its dune,
its place among many.

But Science, he writes, *is the Art of Observation*,
and he places his subject on the counter to watch.

He records the length of its noon shadow, its imprint size
in the butter, how it listens to dreams the way stones listen
to dreams, how long it takes to roll from the bowl lip
to bowl center.

Sinks in water. Quickly, he records. *Stone gravity*, he notes.
All the tests say stone. Except

the test of his hand. There, it is sand from a place
that breezes warm and bows branches over ripeness.
Evidence, he writes, *is a measure of what cannot*

be overcome by Measure. And in this way
he cannot conclude.

Tell me, he begs of the gods, *for I cannot do this alone.*
To comfort him, the gods hide the grain from him
and say they would allow his answer to be as he declares it.
Of course the man will not be consoled this way
and refuses his dinner, recalls how vulnerable

it was in the shadow of a crumb, how it gritted
against its test on glass, recalls the stillness of its patience.
Dust to dust, say the gods. *Let it go.*
But the man dreams of stone mazes and the sand he trails
to escape.
              On waking in the dark, his walls rise up,
but his hands are empty. *Sand*, he groans. *All along,*
it was sand.

But now it is lost and certainly too small
to stand against the wind, which, he notes, is shaking
the long pods of the catalpa and scattering their dust.

3.
After the man lost his would-be stone, his could-be
grain of sand, he made its absence his new study.
Where it had been, he planted a temple of grass.

The grass grew to cover the space of the thing it was not.
Its roots were a permanence the sand never had,
though its greenness could not remain.

Grass was one absence.
Wherever the grain of sand was not became another.
Soon the absences spilled from the bowl, which was one absence,
and onto the table, absence too. It expanded to include the silver,
the food atop the plates. Slipped into cupboards, slept
in the napkins. Each night, the man ate more of this nothing.

The Absence, wrote the man, *now fills the Room.*
I opened the oven and other Sealed Spaces, and
found it there as well. Proof
it has likely been stone all along. For how,
he queried, *could a tiny Grain of Sand fill a space like this?*

He noted that the stone's absence was what he drove over
on his way to the ocean and once he arrived
it was the water as well. Going home he filled his tank with it,
at home it was his pillow and his wife.

Stone, declared the man in *The Book of Various Studies*.
It is a Stone the size of its astonishing absence.

However, said the gods, *if it's as big as you say,*
why can't you find it? They were like that.

The man remembered a photograph of himself
holding a fish close to the camera
so it would appear much larger than it really was.
Then he felt something in his eye

and blinked. *That*, sobbed the man, *is what I'm trying to say*.

THE PERSON WITH THE LOUPE

When the person with the loupe was assigned
to our town, we asked what we could expect
from whatever happens next, but the person
with the loupe wasn't ready to say, so we walked
the sidewalks home, swept the stairs of our entries,
and waited.
        Later, the person with the loupe
was seen examining a building which we thought
was still standing; we all nearly agreed it was,
but the person with the loupe said we weren't qualified.

We could not be accurate to the same degree
as the person with the loupe.
        With the loupe,
it could be determined how much the wind had eroded
the building, the wear from pigeons' feet,
whether the brick could stand up
to whatever time was left.

For anything we needed to know, we were to ask
the person with the loupe.
        The person with the loupe
is always invited. The person with the loupe
does not need to knock and is squinted
from so much looking through.

The person with the loupe prefers stillness to achieve accuracy.
It takes time to be accurate, and we were told
this is what makes it difficult to keep up on things,
as time is an agent of change, and change means something
has moved and will need to be examined.

> Given this,

the person with the loupe is still working
on last year, says,
Each calendar day is a square
the size of all the others.

But the days we recall best seemed otherwise: some shifted long
while others shadowed fast.
Nevertheless, says the person with the loupe.
And, *Therefore*, we are to answer back.

> The person

with the loupe gets the front seat. And is looking at
something we cannot see from here.
From the wrong end of the loupe, we can grow
very far away. We feel we have always been very far away.

IT'S ONLY A LITTLE
LIKE YOU MAY HAVE HEARD ABOUT

They gave me a coat because we'd heard
it was cold out there. Before I left, we recited the numbers
of chill and bite, the equations of freezing.

But once I got out, it was spring. I know
the breeze was not a swan, but it opened its feathers
to me. Opened summer, opened sky, opened next.

What they'd told me no longer bundled neatly.
I was supposed to find the thing they sent me out for
so I could take it back to the examination table
where we could lay it open as a property.

But I didn't find it. Nothing felt
the way I'd been told it would look. I chose a candle.
I think it was called a candle. *It looks like candle,*

but feels like greasy soapstone, I told them
into the mouthpiece. They adjusted the headset.
It's for emergencies only, I said. They asked if I had witnessed
the emergency. They said they could be satisfied

with a measurement. They made a suggestion,
and said I was to return, but I could sense the flowers
might be burned by an oncoming season
and needed me. I would need to watch unobserved.

The candle had a black wick, and this made sense
as I darkened my face in an alley.

LINEAR

The tracks of geese begin with feathers,
the brush of wings against the ground or snow.
Winter is so fast this year
each morning begins with the wreckage of ice, thin around
the bodies of the geese it fastens to the lake.
Footprints of mice begin and end
in weeds whose tops the snow won't take.
The number of footprints is a way to see
how much of their winter fat is making it,
of how many mice have enough left over.
Their tracks are how I see the animals
without me. But sometimes, the turkey
is a whole body against the snow,
and everywhere the deer is a white tail of flight.

ON WHICH THE LOUPE IS FOUND ADEQUATE

The loupe's resolution was determined to be
of the proper kind, and the person with the loupe was found
qualified. For the test, the person with the loupe assessed
the fitness of a building by evaluating the thumbprint
on an air duct.

Overall tension could be seen in the pattern
of seasonal torque. We read the reports
and saw the diploma through glass. When we are asked
if we like this new loupe, we ask how it works.

They explain that when the loupe goes one way, minutia
grows large. When it is turned the other,
minutia disappears
and needs not be answered to.

It should make sense to us
that what is small can either become larger
or disappear. When we are told to accept it,
we are reminded this is how we got here: we were small
but became larger. Remember

how the loupe located grit in the teeth of the thing
we were not to speak of, but which needed
to be buried? Remember how the loupe turned to small,

and the matter of what was missing disappeared?
The loupe came with a manual. Before, we used dreams
to interpret how to speak
to each other; we used clouds and birds.

The loupe cannot see the dreams: they do not exist.

The loupe sees that clouds
are beyond our reach, and so abandoned them.

The birds have proven more difficult,
as they seem to exist but get both near and far.
The loupe is still turning one way
and then another to determine the whether-
ness of birds.

This takes some time, which we are grateful for,
as until it is declared we will be free to wonder.

BAD ADVICE

The empty cage could mean
the rabbit is near, or that there is no rabbit.

If the rabbit is near, then fence the lettuce,
get the camera, tether the dogs, gather the neighbors,
beat the weeds, post a reward.

If no rabbit, options are limited: buy a rabbit,
make a rabbit from chicken wire and leaves,
burn the cage.

Most people prefer the rabbit
even if it is missing.

The rabbit prefers the rabbit.
No rabbit prefers no rabbit. Few people
who do not see a rabbit think to prefer

no rabbit. This is why
even an empty cage turns out to be necessary.
This is why it is poor advice to burn the cage.

THE LOST MAN MEETS THE PERSON
WITH THE LOUPE

From our porches we saw the man enter
our town, stumbling like he'd had the drink
we needed. His face sifted our air, searching
for who knew. We called the person with the loupe.

Who is he, we asked the person with the loupe.
You assume he exists, the person with the loupe replied. *First,
have him stick out his tongue*. But inside
the man's mouth flapped an emptiness
we waited to understand.
There is nothing here, said the person with the loupe,
I cannot work with this.

The man made a frame with his hands, held them
to his chest. We extended his arms
so the person with the loupe could look through:
the frame showed our own skyline, and we
were reminded this was nothing
new, that it had already been recorded
in our *Book of Skies*.

As we led him to the edge
where the trail out had not faded, his breath

rushed out sweetly, not black like the inside.
We were not sure whether to have it noted.

When he left, he bowed low, which was strange,
as we'd given up our kingdom some time ago.

AT THE WEAPON SHOW

At his booth, no guns, no knives
or grappling hooks or Chinese stars. Instead,

on the table he has placed his heart.
With a grip that fits my palm like the muzzle
of a sheep, the heart trembles in my hand.

When I look into an atrium, a night
inside reveals.
Its universe falls open, then pulls back
until its last star contracts
while another galaxy begins. *Now,*

the man explains, *it's everything or nothing.*
No one knows in that kind of dark.

The heart goes on as the man reaches
to settle my throat around its swallowing.
The universe in there is becoming
whatever it can make from the little bit
of light and breath vapor trickling in.

But it's not enough to see by yet.
No way for the people
who will grow their eyes in there
to see the streets they turn down.

AS IF I HADN'T WORN IT QUITE ENOUGH, TIME TATTOOS MY ARMS AND FACE

The lung is one way to enter a tree:
exhale, and breath makes a shadow.
The tree breathes back a dress of vapor.
It is not necessary to wear much more
than that. Not when the body prints
its headline of loneliness on the bed:
Something Broke Here.

Exposure is made of light. A filigree lace
that hangs to dry on the air, my breathing
was meant to insulate me from the world
pressing itself all over everything—
like a little lingerie between what I hoped for
and the rest of it: machines, cowboys, hospital
breakage, motels, bags tossed from the car,
loose hands that confirm the cross references
of someone else's desire.

What am I if not a portrait
of inhabitation? My body assembles
in the light: pinhole, curtain slit, keyshaft
of the onlooking. It takes so little
to be inhabited. Exposure, and each cell surges
to what called forth our first eyes, the first
blooming of peonies and foxgloves,
the fanning-open of leaves,
which I hear and answer in breath.

I have not asked for more than my share.
I want to be answered when I ask, which means
to be dressed by breath, assembled
by light, and admitted into the history of trees.

THE LOST MAN THANKS THE CURTAINS

Under the window of a house where the lost man waits
for darkness, he thanks the curtains for closing
from within: at last, night can undress the world
at its leisure, unfastening bodies
from what the light holds them to.

Outside, the lost man stretches until his arms disappear.
Trees exhale water on the moon.
When the curtain is pulled aside for a moment, the bodies
of flowers and rocks snap back to the shape
of their day forms.

                And then the curtain
is dropped again and holds light's spill
inside, returning the outside world to breath and merge,
delivering the lost man to the cell of his first dividing,
night deer given a body so vast they disperse
into the dark eye of their looking.

The lost man understands the problem with the body
is that it exists. He has seen
that though the body is our own, it can be removed from us.

When he can see his body, it is what he is reduced to.
When it disappears, he owns where it might arrive.
Trees sweep stars into little bundles.
Grasses rise impossibly from the burn.

His children had slept with a light on
so their bodies would stay where they left them.

Burial is nowhere as good as night, as burial only contains
what night releases. Now,

when the lost man leans against dark houses,
it is the same as entering:
he breathes as the house does, breathes as the sleep-
loosened family, as the lilies in the beds, as the settle
of rafters, the cat and her water.

He enters a deeper shadow to unbind himself
from having no place to put his body. When he breathes
where stars go dark, he is received.

3.

WHICH PARTICLE THE PARTICLE

The men in the machine adjust the dials
of the supercollider, anchored at the end
of a tunnel carved through the layers, through the giant
turning of time, the millicellular of what we are made:
dust, orbited speakings, enzymatic pulses
and cursory blips of one receptor to the other.
The men adjust their white coats in that hole,
remember winter as the caves they carved
through drifts, the collapse at one end filling
their mothers with breath and clawing down
and wringing from their guts: *not my baby, god
no, somebody call the trucks.* And the kids crawled out
the other side.
　　　　　　　Then grew up to study
what can happen if we look far enough back
to see the beginning of ourselves.

The men have to find our past from the vantage of now,
a caveat, as most of everything we want to know
about is not-now—*now* being a balance
of one part leading up to, one part away, a hinge
between context and next. The men in the coats
can't wait for next, so must go back
to find the answer to everything.

First, they'll flip a switch. Then something
will happen. On the radio one of them is delivering
the scenario of the barely hypothetical—
of how when they hit the switch each particle
in the universe could become identical
to what it is next to: stranglets.
Right now,

the radio waves of that idea pass through me,
imprinting every cell with news of the oncoming
barely-possible: we will become what we are next to.
As in, if I am washing lettuce when they flip
the switch, I-lettuce. Or if they do it
while I hear the news, I-radio? I-news? Which begs
the question, if I become my husband, pass
through (among?) him, as he will me,
as we filter (are filtered by?) the logs of the house
we fold our clothes in, the nearby detergent, rabbit,
dog, cords, ten of spades, popsicle castle, camera string,
freezer full of beef and goat . . .
Will this save us?
                    I don't mean my husband and me,
but the big us—the world I love? Will I become
the long bean of the catalpa? The snail?

A flipped switch, and—*poof*—Oneness. Just like that.
Finally. This is what we want, I think. Otherwise
the plastic Buddhas and grass-like mats wouldn't be
selling so fast in the department store's Serenity Sale
where you can "Get in touch with your yinner yang."
Then again, our world is hardly made
of what we see, is not catalpa/snail/thing.
Is more vibration/vapor/hum.

Sheila says emotions exist measurably,
that if we deny them their expression,
they simply hitch themselves to our peptides,
ride around, gather other feelings to themselves,
and don't let go until we free them by feeling.
When the men in coats turn the supercollider on
to the next setting, their emotions palpable
as the finger on the switch, will we become
that feeling? Enter the stream of emotions
I can't shake and so keep feeling anyway? Abandoned,
lost, recklessly empowered, frightfully overjoyed . . .
The men in coats hypothesize, calibrate a setting,
reroute cable, send messages up from the center:
it is unlikely, but possible, that in a moment the world
will convert to identical particles.

Which particle the particle of the earth's new design?
Will it ripple out, one thing becoming the next?
Then pull back, the thrown stone of the particulate
back to center until end-X and end-Y are equal?
I shall stand next to something I love from now
until the end of my days. In case, in case.

In the car, the same stereo that held the voice
of the scientist now stereos out Dylan Thomas
who says he sings in his chains like the sea.
And my daughter asks *Why he is green*
and dying, and *Is he really dead?*
And will he always be dead?
My answer includes time and youth, eternality
and mortality, knowledge and innocence,
alcohol, the liver, and the brain. Enough already.
She is five years old.

But is he dead? He is green.
But is he dead? He is talking to us now.
But did he die? My love, there are stars collapsing,
and their light is not a gift but they send it anyway,
and will until we are passed through with it,
until we are hummed with the particulate sift
that hazes the shoulders of nests and melons

and oxen and sisters. And maybe this is how
space gives birth to us, by lighting us
until we can travel and know the inside of lung-wet
and the sluice trail of draft and current. *But is he dead?*
My darling, my dear dear: we are often
what we leave behind. *And the chains?* Yes,
those too. All of it. And all of it is already part of the other.
The chains are holding us now? Exactly now.

Which is why nobody who is old can sleep:
which is to say we sleep less as we break
the world further into sections: me here, you there,
others far away. Peace here, war there. But then,
sometimes, we sit down to warm bread and lemon-oil
over romaine, and we get the brain flash
of someone not eating, of the vulture waiting,
and then no sleep will come that night.
And when we love the fern as it uncurls
greenly here, but (*flash*) over there the green
is burned by a blast, again, no sleep.
And me swelling over my girl as her fist
sweetly, loosely catches puffed breaths of sleep
on a night like the others . . . but then I remember:
over there, a crate of chickens traded for a girl
so young she is guaranteed to cure disease.

Then night is unleashed, the giant smash of it,
and no sleep that night either.
                              We won't sleep
until we stop being surprised by one-thing-
connected-to-the-other. Children sleep.
They understand it happens all at once:
the knee bone connects to the sidewalk bone
and the sidewalk bone connects to the skateboard,
and the skateboard was made in China,
and someone is starving there, which is why
we're talking about the food on your plate. Mystery?
Did someone say there is a mystery?
Snap out of it.

                  The mystery
is that we still separate lights from darks
in the wash, that we blink in surprise every time
we feel let in on another connection:
posture is related to pain, pain chooses
our shoes, our shoes gave us our job, and the job
is related to how much we want our lumps
to be found in time. The world webs and warps,
shifts and dimensionalizes in the wake
of our sudden A↔B↔C and on.
Eventually, we're discussing the shock

that we met at all, shared a coffee, fell in love,
introduced some sperm, and then settled in
with armloads of babies, couches, and shirts,
closing the doors to all that world out there.
We may meet that world yet, the men in coats say,
possibly. Hypothetically.

Will we become what we see or what
we cannot see? Will I become my neighbor, or
her bright smell of lipstick? My walls, or the tension
that inhabits them? The eggs, or the silence
around them? When the men flip the switch,
no one will know it, no broadcast from the center.
It is possible we will be ready, standing
next to what we hope to become;
it is possible we will not, but will become new
anyway. Eventually, sifting; eventually,
osmotic retribution, like it or not, becoming
all we hold or hold out against. They say

the chance is remote, unlikely, infinitesimal,
improbable. This would be comforting,
except I used to be a fish. Before that,
a single cell pulsating against wave current,
run through with salt, slick-ringed

in membrane and open to darkness.
Then light, then a heave of land, then cell
split from my cell and later a flagellate tail,
an eye. Cells of my cell, there was more of me
every day. Eventually, trees, and swinging
through trees. Uprightness. Grass was tool,
rock was ax, smile was challenge, and love
was finding fleas in the fur of our sisters.
It was unlikely, all of it, yet here we are, blinking
at each other in the grocery aisles,
reading ingredients, shoes on, holding money
made of codes the light knows how read.

But scientists are not worried: universal flattening,
uni-becoming . . . unlikely. But ask them
one hundred years ago: Will fat cells colonize
the world? Will food require a definition?
Does god reside in the seizure center of our brains?
Unlikely. Remember Walt, who declared
that science is good at the science of stars,
but does not understand the stars? Unlikely?
For the record, I stand deep-tissue glutted
in the fat of the unlikely.
For example, my father's brother married
my mother's sister. My mother smoked to cut

hunger while my father stirred catsup
into his coffee at a diner. For the nutrition, he said.
They carved a house out of a dream
that broke and planted a garden laid with rubber
snakes to keep the rabbits out.
Next, seven babies, then government cheese for all
of us and in shoes so big every step was a two-step,
or so small every step a half. And later
my mother calling on the phone
because the doctors said it wasn't good, what they saw
when they watched my father's heart
on the machine that speaks in the shadow-whoosh
white-light language we can't understand.
But the doctors could, and it was telling them
it's time to crack my father's chest wide
so they can hold his heart and give him a body
full of someone else's blood. His chances?
Who knows.

        But don't you worry, my mother says,
just concentrate for now on your own good life.
Her voice is a cracker on a wet plate.
My father makes it and wakes up knowing me,
though my sister has become his mother,
and he's sure the nurses are plotting

and so needs a gun for his recovery.
We've seen it before, the doctors say:
His head will clear. And it did. It did. This routine
goes on for years, until my father becomes
his medication, my mother becomes all roads
leading to a hospital, my siblings turn
into doctors, and the heart for everyone involved
gives up lust and burn in favor of spike and dip,
gasp and seize, let and go. All of it
incredibly, fantastically, absolutely unlikely.

They may have already flipped the switch?
See how one thing is already so like
the other? The tabloid blondes, the small-town,
one-block crops of Starbucks, the Gap, TGIF,
all pronounced good in this land of ours,
these storefront windows where they force
another tired bulb of desire.

In Valladolid, Yucatan, embroidered dresses
are the women's famous art,
though the dresses now are worn by tourists.
The locals favor polyester. Polyester delivers
the people to our world where, we see,
if they did flip that switch already,

the machine must have been closest to plastic:
catheters, mean-eyed dolls, fiberfill, Disney snow—
all of it plastic—vacation money, drive-through
windows, fingernails, rock walls, the office ficus,
the entryway ficus, tie clips, singing fish,
sippee cups, even the arm of that Army boy
who was sent away, as he says,
To protect or whatever. You want to know
what that boy was grateful for?
A plastic drinking straw when he woke up.
He'd been goddam *thirsty. It was awesome*, he says.
The little bendy thing made water taste so easy.

My friend Becky is told by her ear doctor
that he'd like to inject her face with paralysis
before those wrinkles really get hold.
It's his business on the side. Or, he says,
she might consider going plastic.
She hears him right. Stepford wives, high-rise
tits, mute faces of the altered.
My friend gets it: her face has let him down.
We might all go plastic. Last year alone,
I ingested at least a soda can's worth
of ChapStick, and who-knows-what is in it.
My daughter teethed a rattle so relentlessly

the pellets fell out, and she ate them. Teflon
is peeling, bottles emit themselves into our water,
and Becky should consider going plastic.

In the center, at the core, there is a switch
of the unlikely. I am driving home fast, into this life
I keep thinking I chose, though I remember,
I distinctly remember, a scientist saying
we are synapse and impulse, predictable
as molecules, calculable as shopping lists.
I am rushing past ash trees, spent roses, smashed
deer, and empty Keystone Light. All the while
my daughter in the back seat talking to Dylan
Thomas about death and what it feels like,
about life and, look, on the windshield,
right there, a beetle, spreading out.

4.

THE HEARINGS

Giant squid washed up on the shores
while inland squirrels dropped from wires
onto our streets. There, Sunday drivers sightsee
for neighborhood foreclosures. Something has occurred
inside our radios:

                The governor has reappeared
to explain the squid. His radio voice says he knows what to do
because he was there and we should not worry. Though

on television it looks different: deep feral eyes
and tight gaspings of unbelief at our upper world,
heat waves prying shadows from their bodies.

It is predicted people will crowd in tight for a better look.

The governor says nothing can go wrong as long as
the vendors keep selling food
and the inspections reveal how things shifted to allow
them passage from their world into ours.

He says, *Yes, we must always assume this might lead*
to a trail of evidence.
Says, *Look for a flier followed by*
An Event. Assume flies. Plan for weather. Stockpile water.
Families will be expected to comment.

During the parade, the gelatinous edges shrank and hardened.

The insides collapsed from the disuse of valves.

It will be days before the office opens and we can ask

to see the original footage.

IN THIS PLACE, WHICH WE HAVE BEEN

Before the people deliver themselves, they want to know
who will become the beetle, who
the sweeper of beetles.

The fish scale in the newspaper is revealing
itself as one of life's previous apples.

The hollow fur of the bear was the first milk
of the untethered goat, looking for something
that wants.

I carried a jar of moths from one day into the next,
wondering if a leaf fallen from the madrone
was the voice of asking to let them go,
the voice telling me I had once been a season.
I let them go.

In the place where one thing is always to become
another, day is night easily, but not before
it is a thousand something elses in between.

Small glaciers shrink from the water in my cup,
sand meets itself in my glass. Tell the pear
not to fear the grass. They have known each other

all this time: once on a ship bearing roots and silk,
once on a train moored by its night of coal.

THE LOST MAN INTERPRETS A CODE

When my husband drops a knife on his toe,
the lost man doesn't know what to do.
The lost man has learned not to talk
about what matters, or it will disappear.
He also learned not to talk about what doesn't matter,
or it will remain.

When I ask the lost man to look at the toe, to get something
for the blood, he assumes I must be using code
for what I am not saying—it can't be that easy.

My husband's toe, I say, *is injured*.
The lost man nods anxiously, wants to play along, looks
for a correlating signal to key the code by.
My husband moans in the kitchen, pointing down. Ah—
the lost man winks to let me know he's got it:
my husband is pointing down. Therefore,
toe means *whatever-is-under-the-floor*.
Bleeding has yet to be established.
The lost man awaits the clue.

The lost man is right, of course—there is something
going on, and though we've been looking away for most of it,
this time, *bleeding* is code only for *bleeding*.

We should have seen the onslaught of these times coming:
when the guard patted down my three-year old
at the airport; when the people in the break rooms
of information extraction stopped discussing
whether the sound this time was more like the scraping
of a chicken or the detangling of a root;
when the leaders couldn't recall.

When I tell the lost man not to worry, that I'll just use
a towel, he presses into the corner, waiting
for the doors to be ripped apart so we can make a choice
about who will go first. *It's just a toe,*
my husband tries to assure him, *no bigger than a pickle.*

But pickle was the wrong word: it means there's no good way
out of this one. We stare at the floorboards: it is still
happening underneath, and to all of us.

COUNTING THE DEAD

One is how it begins. And then, one
again, further over, by someone
else. Turning the body, a worker calls, *This one's
a child*, while another says, *This one's a stone*.
The living call for help carrying their reflections,
brushing the sand from the face of the one
whose body is a shelter of stone.

The clothes blown open as a blister, feet gone,
hands gone, the swarm of flies drone
a song of hunger, each egg a note the dead didn't count on
learning. (One—)

Keep in mind: the beetle is burrowing, *(one)*
the bird is blind from the gorge, *(one)*
the boar will not wait for evening. *(one)*
In the plenty, the animals will not be hungry: *(one)*
the sky of wings, the forest edged in fur. *(one)*
They are filled, one by one by one.

Among the people who stand, the counting continues: *One.*
As an echo others answer: *One.*
Each body infinitely of the first, each to someone
the only one who will not return. This one
the baker, that one the aunt. One
multiplied is one, added is one
more, and missing, one again, but less.

THE LOST MAN WITH DUST

Years after they'd been taken away,
the lost man came across his family as dust
in the corner of the dining room. No wonder
it'd taken so long to see them there:
he'd been eating at the window, waiting to receive.

When he found them, he understood at once
that they had come to him together. *Children*,
he hummed to them, *Uncle, Sister*.
He clapped a ball of dust into the air
then watched the light-charged filter of swift stars
whose patterns he could nearly decipher.

Some of the particles disappeared beyond
the strip of light and were lost again to him.
He swept up what he could and widened
the curtains so the light could hold them longer.
My babies, he hummed, *my only onlies*.

He understood that the force of his breath, no matter
how he softened it, would both give some
and take some from the raft of light. He thought about this
as he breathed in the dust-charged air and wept, breathed
and praised the falling constellations.

THE LOST MAN DISAGREES WITH THE CLOUDS OUT OF PRINCIPLE

On the hill where clouds gather and disperse
the lost man argues with them about how to remain.
The clouds shift, telling him transience,
asserting ephemera and next.

The lost man wants to believe he is a stone
of what has happened already, that he may become
a monument of what will come.
The clouds render wisps as he acts out his everness
for them. He shows them how to stay,
meditates solidity while they mackerel and yawn.

The clouds have seen things.
When the lost man asks how to have enough
to last what is left of him, the clouds shrug,
answering cryptically with a fish-into-shoe.

The lost man shrugs back—he doesn't get it,
so the clouds try again: a cloud heap gets swept
into the clean ocean of sky, a cloud sweater shrinks,
a puff of deer head watches an unraveling doll
consume the world. The clouds flatten themselves
to ask if he understands it yet.

But the lost man has seen things too. He points
to a cloud eye opening, then to his own eye which watches.
But when he blinks, the cloud's eye swells itself
shut for good.

Still, it feels so good to have someone to speak with
in the shapes of things that the lost man is afraid
to weep, as it may result in a misunderstanding of rain.

Instead, he composes a house of air,
opens the front door, and sits inside. When the wind
rips at his clothing, he opens a window
to let it through. When the clouds strip themselves
from the sky, the lost man pulls the shades.

THE MAGICIAN

Without using the words infinity
or talon, without feral
or the phrase stars like teeth
in the neck of night. Without bone.
No moss or aperture. The wrist
absent of flourish and the cup
of milk without a motive.
A palimpsest so thin it is the text.
Away the moon and how light
allows the morning. Perhaps light.
No body undulate. Perhaps body.
Without the declivities of collarbones,
the rustle of want. Come to me.

THE PERSON WITH THE LOUPE
CONFIRMS THE CHILDREN

When the convoy came into town in their trucks,
they took whomever came down off the porches, except
for the person with the loupe. The children were the ones
who went down, as the person with the loupe had said
we might expect.

     Children cannot stay on porches long
when trucks drive slowly past with flashing lights
and telegraphing god in a melody where everything
is round. Children are drawn to roundnesses. They went
down. Dogs went down but were untouched.
The distinction was noted by the person with the loupe.
The woman with a flowering hedge went down to urge
the children back,

     and we understood this was her choice.
At first it felt strange without so many of us left
because we are usually given most of the rules ahead of time:
senior-sale Tuesdays, Wednesday buffet
at five, wear shoes, cross at your turn, bury
what should not come back.

     Our town was thinned,
though the lawns stayed trimmed and the bus stopped
as usual. Eventually the children were returned, taller,
but the dogs recognized them by failing to bark,
and the person with the loupe's scale confirmed
they had received their calories daily and on time.

Their new language was made out of our own words
but meant differently.
                              The person with the loupe
called out their names from memory,
and we were grateful for this, as the list had gone missing,
and no one else was sure of how to know them.

LOW RENT

When the grocer's eye socket is vacated
by his eye, there is an eye's-more of room
in the apartment of his head,
and the landlord demands more rent.
The grocer insists he shouldn't have to pay:
It's not my fault some kid's toy exploded in my eye.

But the landlord is adamant—he's knows
he's got a good thing: he went
to the local landlord meeting and they told him
it'd be like this: the grocer whining
about due diligence and maintenance fees,
imminent domain and how it isn't his fault
and yah yah yah.

Anyone can see the property
the landlord is talking about:
the extra room opened up in the man's head
which our gazes pry into like bad neighbors.
We want it cleaned up.
We want the crummy lid reopened
and the smell gone, along with a timeline
and an explanation for when and how.
The landlord explains to the grocer
that all this attention is worth something.

The grocer wants to see
the list of comps, so

the other landlords of lost legs and hands
help out, and the list is drawn up.
Seems unfair, sighs the grocer,
that my eye is so low rent—I've seen some amazing things
from there.
The landlord expected this:
Yeah, but that's not what people are looking at now—
they all see what you won't.

There isn't a way around it. The grocer pays up
and the landlord provides the hole with a patch.
At night, the grocer turns off the lights
and raises that darkness,
allowing it to be replaced by one far larger.
It's really more than he's paid for,
that expansive, gigantic lawn of night,
though sometimes we ourselves open
the window and allow in certain parts of the evening
that are well beyond our means.

IN THE HOTEL OF DESIRE'S RECEIPT

In the hotel's lobby, I am refused
nothing. There will be a storm at eight, a stone
angel will appear heavily and grant wishes
on the veranda, and the staff encourages us to hold
the nearest stranger tenderly
until winter's bus departs.

In the lobby, I may receive the phone call
from the brother who will tell me his child's
name, and hunger is a pet that feeds itself.
Huddling with our heads bowed is not necessary.
When we check in, parts of the sky are named
for us, and our pockets are filled with coins to spend
on forgetting.

The clerks compliment our names
as stars wait behind a screen of sky for us
the way stones wait to rise from the hills.

The phone is ringing. Whatever happens next,
there will always have been first the ringing of that phone
and the room's sudden freezing until it is answered,
the voice at the other end which might say anything
into a room where the answer must be yes.

Before the angel grants the wishes, admits the clerk,
it actually could land anywhere.

IMPOSSIBLE TO KNOW
WHICH RING THE RING OF THE ANSWER

The trees comb out my questions
until the words are so straight the little climb
and lift of each letter's sound goes singular and stranded.

Trees like it best when the question is not specific,
prefer the charge of pure asking
which they do not pretend they can address by anything but time.

One of the trees translates
the years of beetles. Another unwinds a cloud.

What I needed from them got snagged on the branch
of a fir. The sack of it torn and spilling.

The tree may get to it some generation: but for now
there is still the ice age they need to declare, and they suspect
one of themselves is thinking again of fire.

The trees are not catching up. They are not behind.
Time is not for the trees, just as the river
is not for its stones.

Last week, a pheasant saw me and went still
in the unanchored shadows of the trees. The trees confuse us
all the time. To them, all asking the same asking.

THE LOST MAN LEAVES A WILL

To the wind, the fullness of my mouth, juice
of my openness. To gnawing things, the osseous fists
of my bones' rebinding. I want the earth
to accept my head. I have wanted to be held
by something my entire life, something that demands
all of me to answer back with holding.

To my gone children, all I cannot say without
my tongue. I call you in silence. You answer
in kind, and are counted. To birds, a nest of hair
and threads for the wobble-necked and pink-bodied.

I give the trust of grass to bear and raccoon,
to the crepuscular world who pauses before taking,
whose staring eyes give back the light of cars
as if to fix the breakage of air
before the great coming down upon them.
I have been broken. I
have been broken.

My walk from one place to this did not leave
a trail: I walked my route only once, and once-
forward is not enough to be remembered by grass.
My path is where I column into my own shape.
I give space to air with my leaving.
I give space to flying with my leaving.

I ask for nothing in return. I have already received
more than this, and worse: the world afloat; answers
at once and for nearly everything; animal bellies
untethered and dragging.

To the leaf, serration of my teeth.
To water, ice of my witnessing. It will need it.
To deer, asking and then emptiness before slaughter.
The grass should take my memory. But to the trails worn
by the escaping many, the mud of unknowing.

Here is what I know for now: worms,
I have loved you rightly
since I learned that dirt holds secrets blind and dependent
on whatever mercies we are willing to gift. I gave you names.
I counted your rings, measured your body-yawns

toward darkness. Worms, you are better than stars
because you are here.

                    Do you remember
how my mother stitched her people's names
to my cuffs and then disappeared? The birds left
before the people did, but you, you worms, you stayed.

To the worms, my thanks. I ask you to make me rich
within yourselves: you stayed. While the earth
was fleeing itself, I named you, and you answered
to the place of my naming, and remain.

FOUR LAKES POETRY SERIES
Ronald Wallace, General Editor

Taken Somehow by Surprise • David Clewell

Help Is on the Way • John Brehm

The Declarable Future • Jennifer Boyden